Transplants

poems by

Pat Butler

Finishing Line Press
Georgetown, Kentucky

Transplants

Copyright © 2017 by Pat Butler
ISBN 978-1-63534-146-1 First Edition
All rights reserved under International and Pan-American Copyright Conventions.
No part of this book may be reproduced in any manner whatsoever without written permission from the publisher, except in the case of brief quotations embodied in critical articles and reviews.

ACKNOWLEDGMENTS

"Transplants," *Vivid Magazine,* OM Arts Intl., Vol. 2, Issue 2, Tyrone, GA, October 2016
"Titus the Titmouse," Honorable Mention, PeachJam Poetry Competition, Friends of the Peachtree City Library, 2013 Poetry Competition; published in *Peachtree Poets 2015* Peachtree City Library, Inc., Peachtree City, GA, 2015.
"A Conversation in Autumn," originally published as "Our Wabi Sabi World," First Place, Friends of the Peachtree City Library 2013 Poetry Competition; published in *Peachtree Poets 2013* Peachtree City Library, Inc., Peachtree City, GA, 2013.
"The Importance of the Hummingbird" and "Planting Seeds," Honorable Mention, National Poetry Month Poetry Competition 2011, Friends of the Peachtree City Library; published in *National Poetry Month* April 2011, by Friends of the Peachtree City.

Publisher: Leah Maines

Editor: Christen Kincaid

Cover Art: Photographer: Pat Butler

Author Photo: Garrett A. Nasrallah

Cover Design: Elizabeth Maines

Printed in the USA on acid-free paper.
Order online: www.finishinglinepress.com
also available on amazon.com

Author inquiries and mail orders:
Finishing Line Press
P. O. Box 1626
Georgetown, Kentucky 40324
U. S. A.

Table of Contents

Branch In The Fog 1

Driving South, Driving Slow 2

The Great Machipongo Clam Shack 4

Deptula Road 6

On Buying A Couch 7

Titus The Titmouse 8

Transplants 9

Red Barn 10

Frog 11

The Night The Moths Came In 12

A Poem Of Hours 13

A Slow Poem 14

The Great Peach State Blizzard 15

The Snow Candle 16

Spoons 17

Red Clay 18

Gay Pride Weekend 19

The Importance Of The Hummingbird 20

Planting Seeds 22

Or I Can Stand Here Forever 23

The Uninvited Goat 24

A Conversation In Autumn 26

In honor of the Great Peach State, and its good people, where I spent many good years.

"*My people will live in peaceful dwelling places, in secure homes, in undisturbed places of rest.*"
—*Isaiah 32:18*

BRANCH IN THE FOG

holds onto the leaf,
like the two it takes
to hold on:
the one that holds firm,
if the other lets go.

DRIVING SOUTH, DRIVING SLOW

I toy with a prayer on the roof of my mouth—
it bats like a moth; wings thrash to get out.

Paying the toll for the interstate south, more
questions than answers, more faith than doubt,

I roll down the window and turn up the sound.
If I don't hear my name, I might turn around.

I'll look for my name, driving south, driving slow,
ears cocked to the crows on Magotha Road.

I'm turning the corner on I know not what—
will you tell me, crows, what it is you know?

Traffic is moving, though a lane is closed;
I take the next exit—the scenic route.

Do I drive too fast to hear my name?
Who am I now, in the far right lane?

Will I hear my name on the Chesapeake Bay?
Will it sound like thunder, lightning or rain?

Will the gulls drown it out, or the hum in the tunnel?
Will the live oaks know it, or the Spanish moss?

Have I ears to hear, and a heart to change?
The questions give way to salt marsh and sand.

The camellias in Richmond remind me of home.
I stop for lunch on Rehoboth Road.

In North Carolina, the kestrel spires
over sullen trailers, a junkyard pile.

Charleston turns its head away;
if Savannah knows, it does not say.

On Tybee Island, the bald eagle waits
with impeccable patience, the raptor's pace.

If I heard my name, I'd be no one's prey.
I'd know what to do, know what to say.

Consider the cotton and acres of pine;
you never know when you've crossed a line.

Slave shacks straggle into view—collapsed
and burned—the crape myrtles mute.

If I heard my name,
I could be free.

If I heard my name,
I'd know what to do.

When You call I would answer
like a moth to flame.

I would know how to answer
if I heard my name.

THE GREAT MACHIPONGO CLAM SHACK

Driving up Route 13 in Nassawadox, VA,
just north of the Chesapeake Bay,
we're hungry for seafood.

THE GREAT MACHIPANGO CLAM SHACK
looms on a billboard

followed by JUST SEAFOOD—
    followed by CLOSED FOR THE SEASON—
        followed by MOVED.

We note the dripping red arrow, painted
like a bloodthirsty fish hook, pointing left
past Yuk-Yuk & Joe's BBQ Grill, Stuckey's Fireworks,
and *yes!* The Great Machipango Clam Shack is *not*
closed for the season!

We wander in among oysters, bayside beauties,
and seaside salts, 50 or 100 count bags,
shucked, cooked, peeled, deveined.

A waitress elbows her way through swinging doors:
pert as a prawn, primping frizzed hair,
spritzed in oyster and lime,
New Zealand accent in her mouth,
black glasses sliding down her ski slope nose,
teeth as wide as the Coconut Crusted Tilapia,
with mango papaya sauce in hand
and a boisterous *Hey!*
Get your omega-3 Fatty Acids here!

Heat and eat your fill of cat fish, claw, calamari,
grouper, fat jimmies, crab cakes or lump backfin.
The Veri Teri Ahi Tuna is grilled and today's

Great Fish Deal. Alligator tail sits with salt cod
and seafood cakes, Upper Crust Gourmet Fish fillets,
ready to cook and serve, instructions included.

Cornbread Crusted Catfish on her collar,
she serves us shrimp and corn chowder,
chives and cheddar on the side.
And leaning in with garlic on her breath,
she counsels: *Any 10 fish—$29.95!*

Ginger ale fizzes up our noses.
We toss our cans in the recycle bin,
ready for the road again, bolstered by
this bayside beauty, and omega-3 fatty acids.
We wave goodbye to her parting:
Doctors say eat fish twice a week!

And pulling out on Route 13,
leaving Nassawadox, VA,
with tuna in our teeth, lemon on our fingers,
and sauce in our spirits,
we smack our lips, digesting the feast.

DEPTULA ROAD

Angling along anorexic pines,
the road I walk in silence
reveals nothing of what's ahead.

Discrete companion of curves,
it ends, and I conclude, to my great
surprise, that I've arrived.

ON BUYING A COUCH

Though I have availed myself of other couches,
armchairs in libraries, or beds in guest rooms—
lamps reading over my shoulder at kitchen tables,
mug in hand, a clock with its man-in-the-moon
message of hours—
                    still, there is nothing quite
like one's own couch, planted firmly in the direction
of pine wood, beach, or sky—to contemplate eternity,
stretch the legs luxuriously, and recalibrate
the uncertainties.

Good to have a companion—to be safely buckled
into a cushioned seat for the hard landings
a phone call can bring, curling the soul into a ball.

Good to have a presence that keeps its peace
while hearing all. Confessional for guests,
and when guests leave, to flop, fit a pillow
under the head, flip a magazine, reclined
and steady under the fan's faint breeze;
to gaze at stars, and know each star is named.

Good to have a couch on which to count
each leaping frog and frantic moth,
the deer frolicking under the pines.
At night to fall asleep, to crickets in tune
with infinite, infinitesimal things, waiting
for the Man in the Moon to rise.

TITUS THE TITMOUSE

In the vineyard, Titus, or one that looks like him,
flits from vine to vine in the first November sun—
from fencepost, page and pen; in sketch book pad, and back again,
to the ripple of oar in lake, the coffee rapidly going cold.

My eyes flit from vine to vine in the first November sun.
I swat a fly, write the icon, wring the odd insight from this vine,
to the ripple of oar in lake, the coffee rapidly going cold.
What is a vineyard after all—but grapes redeeming the apple's fall?

I swat a fly, write the icon, wring the odd insight from this vine,
from fencepost, page and pen, and start a sketch book page again.
What is a vineyard after all—but grapes redeeming the apple's fall?
In the vineyard, with Titus, or one that looks like him.

TRANSPLANTS

The morning glory blooms purple now—
cold lips crimped and quivering
in November's contemptible wind.

Whatever climate it came from,
blown in on the autumn rains,
it shivers now without complaint,
baby blue days of summer gone.

I pull a purple sweater on,
a transplant like this stubborn vine.
I miss the baby blue summer too,
and envy this vine's vigorous root.

In royal colors, it bends and sways;
I haven't the guts for November days.
Before the hard frost falls tonight,
I contemplate its grit and fight.
Intrepid Vine, at the edge of doom,
you teach me to stay.
Teach me to bloom.

RED BARN

Roof angled and pitched for relief,
inviting eyes to rest and see
storehouse and treasury,
tempered with economy,
buffered and weathered by history,
spacious and shuttered,
clapboard and cupola,
aged architecture
atop which a copper
weathervane swivels
north and south.

All is order and efficiency,
a temple of tenacity,
a ripe red apple offered me
as I wobble existentially,
question life's complexity,
falter in perplexity,
and toy, just a touch,
with self-pity.

I bow to this theophany,
grateful for its company,
its color, line and harmony.

And dwarfed by its muchness,
invited to trust,
I approach its treasure,
as yet untouched.

FROG

Somewhere in my house hides a frog.
Crouching under the couch perhaps,
seat of my concern for his whereabouts.
I don't know where he is, or how to get him out.
Surely he knows where he is—
if unsure of how to leave.
So much am I on my couch like this frog:
neither of us finding a way out, both hiding
from the big hand, the dark shadow,
and the sweeping broom, only trying to help.

THE NIGHT THE MOTHS CAME IN

They poured in, like commuters at rush hour in a train station. I rose and ushered them in, inviting them to make themselves at home. The large ones settled high on the white wall, and said nothing, like old uncles. The smaller ones flitted about, no doubt looking for whatever moths bed down in for the night. I let them flit, settling back on the couch to continue my evening, checking occasionally to make sure they weren't getting into mischief.

I don't know what kind of trouble stalked in the pine forest, what caused them to flee as if from a speeding train. I've had to do that myself at times—make myself small against a wall while some terror rode before me.

In the morning, a few were still batting about, crazed, needing air. I hurried to get them outside before they lost their minds completely, or died. Two made it. As for the rest, I can only hope they found a way out through the pipes, cracks, and vents of 125 Logos Way, and are passing the word that safe passage can be found there, unless inadvertently locked in.

A POEM OF HOURS

Sleepless with the night bird's song—
what makes us different from everything else?

At dawn, the crow's caw commands me
to rise—awake, alive.

At nine, a dog barks, a car passes.
What do I have that I did not receive?

At noon the day demands I bring my house
in order. How can I refuse?

At four, the wind chases dead leaves around
my ankles. *Run—as if your life depends on it!*

In the evening, I return home, to the unmade
bed, unsaid prayers, everything left undone.

At night, more stars than darkness cover me,
and the glad deer return.

A SLOW POEM

It drops like an autumn leaf,
escorted by thermals,
a slow descent to the ground,
preparing for Spring.

Not the frank fall of the pinecone,
a hard thud on the stern dirt—

this is the wistful drift,
the pause at the doorway,
a slipping out while no one's looking,
lingering, with a backwards glance
before a pivot, then the soft landing.

Unwritten, it falls, to let another rise;
an unpoem: no words. Hushed
and hidden. A slow poem,
that sleeps through the night,
silent and dormant through winter's
rude bite, that will find its words
next Spring, as surely as the shoot
unfurls to the light.

THE GREAT PEACH STATE BLIZZARD

hit Tyrone on the eve of Thanksgiving,
to the children's delight, the Yankees' derision.
By dawn, the town dozed in a dusting
the northerners could only mock.

The wind howled, like those damn Yankees,
laughing all over town, especially when
the snow plow arrived from Alabama.
It skidded around the park, righting itself
in time for the rising sun,
which promptly began to melt the dust.

Children crafted snowmen (more leaves
than snow, which they used for glue).
Snowball fights were not an option.

The foreigners stared from windows,
confused by the children's attempts,
and the gap between images seen on TV,
and what was (almost) outside on the ground.

Martha ran to the kitchen to grab a spatula
to flick a few flakes from the windshield,
and we braved a trek to the store—
avoiding snow drifts in our minds,
imagining ice on Lake Kedron—

imagining signature drinks we would make
on Thanksgiving,
to toast a thing that almost came, but didn't,
was almost seen, but vanished,
just as we turned to look.

THE SNOW CANDLE

The cashier, curious, promptly opens it,
inhales, and affirms: *It does have a smell!*

Not to diminish its beauty (just try to live
with it!), I answer: *Yes, it does have a smell.*

And: *No, I'm not from here—*
but like my snow this way,

in a jar, a white column like one might find
on a fence post, and knock down—

no resemblance to the real intoxication.
I drive home and place the candle in the window.

A domesticated cat, it purrs a tame storm.
I coax its wick and wax:

Remember Wind!
Remember Blizzard!

With a fragrance more cotton than snow,
it nevertheless warms some home in my bones,

and recalls the silence, the absolutes,
the cold perfection, my hard frost roots.

And to the curious cashier, I would now say:
Move north! Smell real snow!

Then try to live without it.

SPOONS
After "The Miracle Worker"

One and another, another, they drop—
are tossed, thrown, flung with ferocity:
Helen, facing off over spoons with Annie,
and losing.

Later it will be water gushing, slopping over
the two tussling, hair undone, glasses flying,
pitcher filling in spite of itself, like Helen's mind,
making connections. She'll lose again (her prison).

Maternal love will interfere, paternal reason reason,
a bitter brother mock attempts to tame his caged
sibling. None will win against this Teacher,
tenacious as no other.

What spoons are in my hand? What fingers playing
games? What Annie to my Helen claims:
Each thing has a name! There's a word for it!
What light dawns in my mind?

A Voice invades this cage of mine, fingers flying
in my hand. The scales fall, the heart perceives:
Put down your spoons, Caged Prisoner!
Put down your spoons. I have a Name.

RED CLAY

A fine mist polishes the lane,
leaching red clay into puddles and rivulets
streaming around the stop sign,
the Furniture Pro Shop, racing the roan
that now runs to my approaching umbrella,
as if I'm a herald, as if I know something,
or carry the food bucket, or know when it's coming.

Four mares stand in the pasture, riveted,
then stampede over—as if the roan *had* received
something, and I was a herald.

I tell them how beautiful they are, how delightful
the walk, the rain, the quiet, the heron overhead,
the mystery critter that scrambles under the brush.

The mist mixes ochre, sienna, burnt umber—
pine needles bronzed and ready to join
the nut-brown acorns on the ground,
oak and pecan leaves, mottling the earth's floor.

A pack of Camels floats past the Spoon Sisters'
warehouse, past the Red Door Consignment Shop.
The fullness swells, the heron flies, the horses gallop,
and I get it, Red Clay. I get you. I *am* you:
dust to dust, clay from clay, both out here on
a rainy day, content to graze, or float away.

GAY PRIDE WEEKEND

She marches into this alternate fray of humanity,
past booths and balloons, the perfume of buttered
popcorn, pumpkins, candy corn, and costumes
all around this side of the back side of the park,
to see men and women in cotton candy wigs—
Sailor Boy, Super Star, Saved and Gay—sporting
t-shirts that say:
>*I can't even think straight.*
>*[Marriage is so gay.]*
>*You hate us. We hate you.*

What to do?

She sits with the idle, the psychics, the Christians,
the families yearning for absent loved ones nowhere
in this crowd, in another city in fact, but in this city,
Gay Pride Weekend gives them a chance, a face,
someone to hug. They come and commune with people
they hope will transmit that love all the way back to
the city where the absent distant loved one dwells.

She sits, and no one can tell if she's gay or straight—
least of all the man sitting next to her,
wild-eyed with a t-shirt red like bleeding blaring
I can't sleep. Clowns will eat me—
and decides to keep it that way.

THE IMPORTANCE OF THE HUMMINGBIRD

who got trapped in our receiving bay and—
according to Google—had only one hour
to escape before dying of dehydration.

So he quickly opens windows and doors,
turns on lights, and pulls a ladder out,
wondering if he's being ridiculous,
squandering precious time, or saving
the hummingbird, and his soul.

And wielding a large swath of cardboard
then, with which to shoo it out, he worries
that he'll swat too hard, provoking the bird's death,
but if he doesn't swat, and the bird dies…
sin of omission or commission?

Always the same koan and conundrum—
with so little time, and death imminent—
only an hour. He drops to his knees
in an agony of prayer and frustration,

then jumps up, runs to the neighbor
to borrow her hummingbird feeder—
no time for chit chat—and hurries back.

Standing then near the receiving bay,
door open, arm held out straight with feeder
dangling from his finger, he remembers
that doing anything alone for a long period
of time, however minor, can collapse the will.
Still he stands.

And the waiting affords him time to think
and fear failure, faulty judgment, mistakes,
and weigh how barren the busy life, that
questions the importance of a hummingbird.

When such a man does not waver but keeps
his arm out and, with minutes to spare,
the hummingbird finds it,
and, with an instinct to rise, escapes—

I say that this man too has an instinct to rise,
and feel sure that there is an Arm held out a door,
long past reason, in hopes that he will find it,
and escape.

And to this Arm is lashed an Irrevocable Will
that stands, and stands there still.

PLANTING SEEDS

I'm planting seeds in the softened earth
of a Georgian spring, on a quiet Sunday
afternoon, while others hike or hang
with family, talk on phones, or fall asleep—
but these seeds need to go in now.
These seeds are late—I'm long overdue.
If I don't plant now, no flowers will bloom.

I'm new to this land, to the work, the pace;
the garden grounds me with a sense of place.
Will it grace me with profusion?

Here, paucity rules: the terrace small,
the drought prolonged. Sooner or later,
so I'm told, the deer will eat it all.
Still, I plant seeds, and in my same way:
same fingers, same tools, same pots
to prove a previous life existed.

But these seeds go in a different soil now;
the rain is different and (does it show?)
I'm different too.

Do I even know how to write anymore?
I'll plant these seeds, and when I'm done,
pen a few lines and see what comes,
because there is rain today...rain...

OR I CAN STAND HERE FOREVER

Something has pushed up strong and new—
with an infant's cry that will not, I think,
be easily satisfied.

Already refusing complacency, the easy sleep
of stability, it elbows me aside, the small
comforts too, seeking independence.

I thought this spring we would open the porch,
unshutter windows, sweep the cobwebs,
change the wardrobe, and Life could go on.

But the sun climbed up like a child from its crib,
and light shone on another departure
announcing itself.

Already an adolescent, it runs up the hill,
not looking back, and I can smile and wave goodbye,
or stand here forever, weeping.

THE UNINVITED GOAT

She crashes our conference at coffee break,
unmindful of stares, does not care, but comes,
wanders among us, nibbling fingers and thumbs,
snuffling through pockets and poking her nose
up sleeves, looking for whole things—not crumbs—
and one of us succumbs to this young goat
with no sense of propriety, no sense at all.

She must be a she-goat, a Mary Magdalene
school-of-thought goat: no ceremony standing
in the way of what matters.

Without invitation, she begs no permission,
plunks hooves on the table and rummages
through the herbal teas.

I marvel at her ease: how without so much
as a *thank you* or *please*, she helps herself
to whatever she sees.

For protocol she obviously has no use,
and protocol suggests no next move.
Her beard sashays over a gurgling bell
dangling from her collar and matted,
musty pelt. Her thin goat lips tease napkins
from wrappers and chocolates from cups,
as she cocks a square-pupiled eye at the muffins.
Nostrils flare. Abrupt as a sneeze, she bleats
and butts them into the air, and as we laugh,
breaks wind.

She snubs our judgment.

The conference resumes,
but no power point can compete
with this wonder of a goat not aiming to please.
What else could she teach?

We stare out the window as she saunters away,
with a flick of her tail, in her own goat way—
triumphant—as I remember the day.

A CONVERSATION IN AUTUMN

Waxing or waning,
the moon wakes me,
and I run to the window,
or out in the night,
shivering under the stars,
wrapped in a blanket,
staring straight up.

Or at the beach with its whistling wind,
whipping the shorebirds up the shoreline,
ruffling the sea grass, salt marsh and sails.
I watch the run-and-pause of plovers,
the egret fishing, its stick legs.

Have you seen the inside of broken shells?
Have you watched the tide go out?

What about the flowers—their perfumes?

The orphans, their eyes? The iris, in the eye?

All that beauty.

I'm thinking of *wabi sabi*, the death and beauty
of all things incomplete, imperfect, impermanent;
everything withering, rusting, dissolving.

Thinking how, again this autumn, crossing continents,
cultures and time, my addiction to beauty is challenged:
Crucifixion. Auschwitz. A death in the family.

Wabi Sabi confronts me, provokes me, dares me
to confess, make peace with, embrace decline and death.
I can't.

Who, gasping for air, does not seek the open window?

Get outdoors, Wabi Sabi concedes, and capture the image.

I grab my camera.

At first, all I could see was the beauty:
gold trees like lamps in the wet wood,
    water bursting the beaver dam,
        the happy dog with its smiling human,
            the surprise of pumpkins, pomegranates,
                and on the shoals, a bouquet of wilted flowers—

all my heart alive in that beauty.

Nothing lasts.
Nothing is finished.
Is anything perfect?

Not as I traveled in Poland,
with its death camps and butcheries—
or in Hungary, with its quotas and ghostly *shtetls*.
Not last Autumn when my grandmother died,
ashes to ashes, dust to dust.

Is Wabi Sabi right then, with its seed spilled on the ground,
its shroud of vines and detritus, its dead tree trunks?

I bow among the red-berried branches to the cycle
I've lived all my life, and say *No, Wabi Sabi.*

Seed is sown for Spring.

Even death can be beaten,
or Autumn is a lie.

Pat Butler, a native New Yorker, has transplanted to New England, France, and the South, and currently resides in Florida. Transition, transience and relocation are therefore a way of life, and the major theme of this chapbook.

Two previous chapbooks, *Poems from the Boatyard* and *The Boatman's Daughter*, explored themes of place, identity and home. *Transplants* probes the dislocation, disorientation, and emotional dynamics of transition.

The Boatman's Daughter finds herself on a new shore, returning to America after 12 years overseas. America has changed, as has she: a frenetic urban pace slows to small town rhythms; the hustle of the city relaxes into contemplations on the couch. Northern directness, mellowed by French finesse, now yields to Southern charm. The poems, written mostly in Georgia, observe its culture, wildlife and rhythms, through the lens of re-entry shock. Transition is eased by the gifts of magnolias, hummingbirds, and soft temperatures.

Transplants opens with a poem that evokes the emotional roller coaster of transition, and closes with one that resolves its tensions. Both poems are set, appropriately, in Autumn, the season that marked the anniversary of Pat's arrival in and, eight years later, departure from Georgia. The season appears as one of the chapbook's main characters, with its distinctive rhythms of death and release, gathering and harvest. It provides an apt metaphor for transition, and ultimately reveals where hope can be found.

This is Pat's third chapbook with Finishing Line Press. She has also been published in a number of literary and online journals, including *Cardinal Flower, Aurorean,* and *Ruminate*. Pat is part of the Peachtree Poets' scene, including its annual poetry competition, where she has won numerous awards, mentions, and publication in their chapbooks; four entries appear in *Transplants*.

Follow Pat on social media and the following sites:

Website: www.theliteraryboatyard.wordpress.com
Blog: http://poemsfromtheboatyard.blogspot.com/
Facebook: Poems from the Boatyard
Instagram: boatyardpat

www.ingramcontent.com/pod-product-compliance
Lightning Source LLC
LaVergne TN
LVHW041514070426
835507LV00012B/1564